NOTE-FOR-NOTE
KEYBOARD
TRANSCRIPTIONS

DREAM·THEATER

Selections from
THE ASTONISHING

Music transcriptions by Chris Romero

ISBN 978-1-4950-7176-8

HAL·LEONARD®
7777 W. BLUEMOUND RD. P.O. BOX 13819 MILWAUKEE, WI 53213

T0056120

In Australia Contact:
Hal Leonard Australia Pty. Ltd.
4 Lentara Court
Cheltenham, Victoria, 3192 Australia
Email: ausadmin@halleonard.com.au

Visit Hal Leonard Online at
www.halleonard.com

Dystopian Overture

Music by
John Petrucci and Jordan Rudess

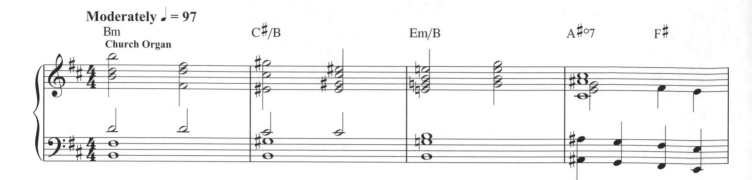

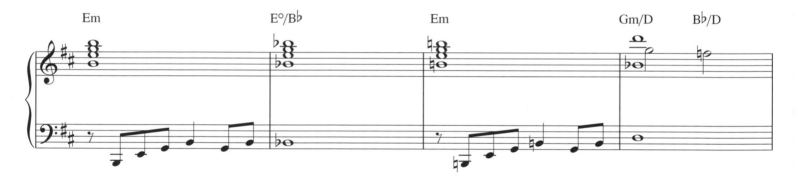

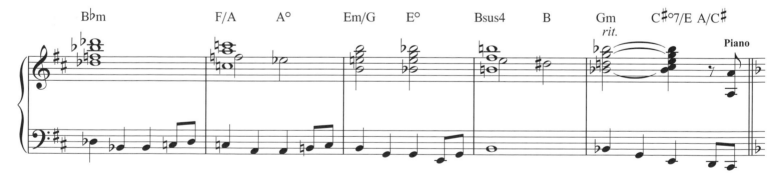

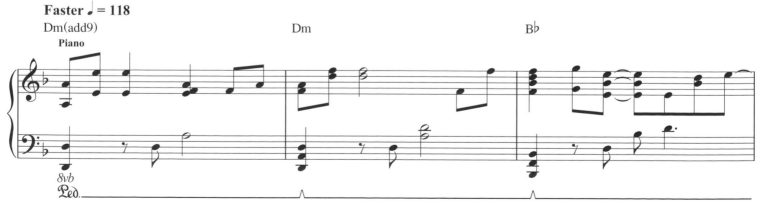

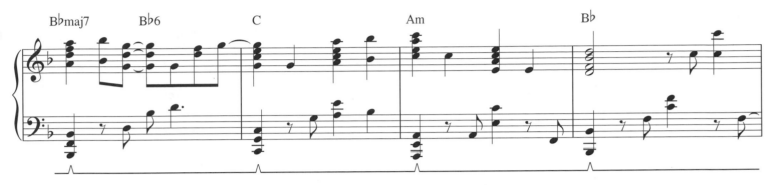

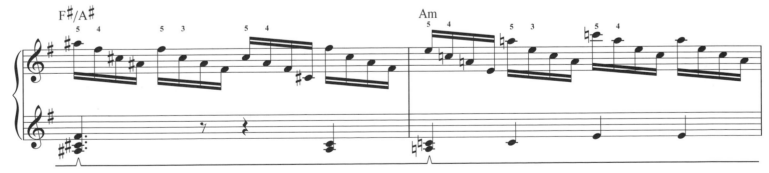

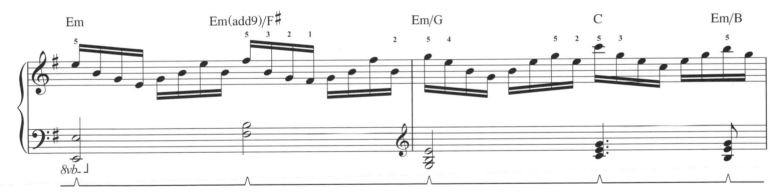

4

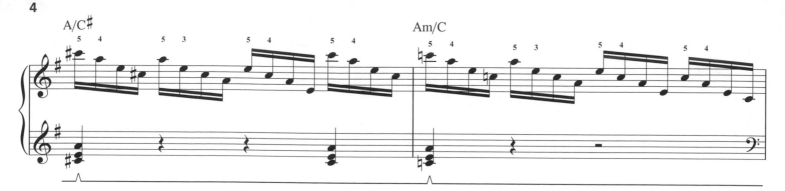

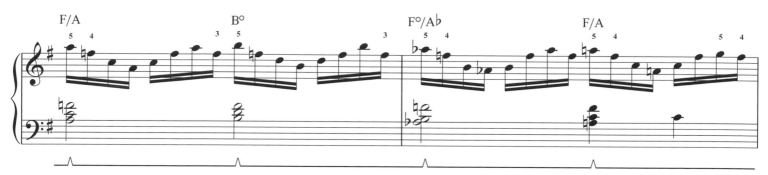

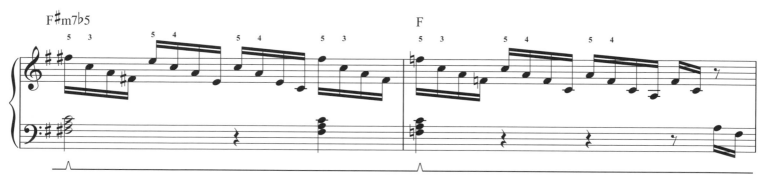

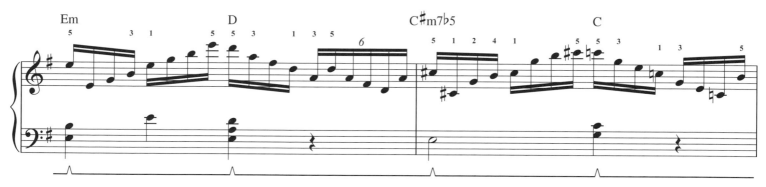

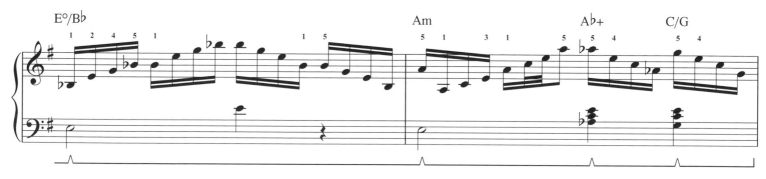

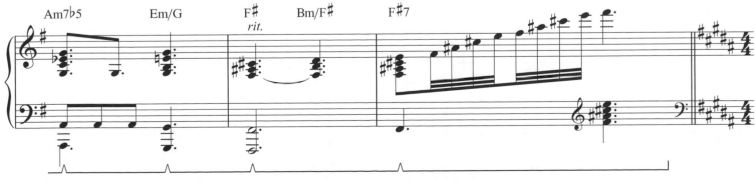

Slower ♩ = 116

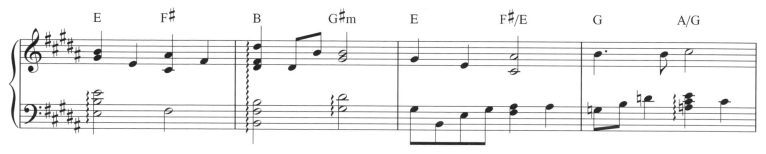

Slower ♩ = 90

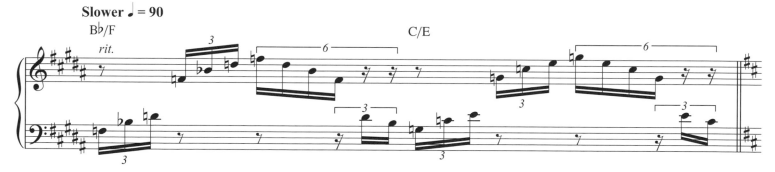

Faster ♩ = 116

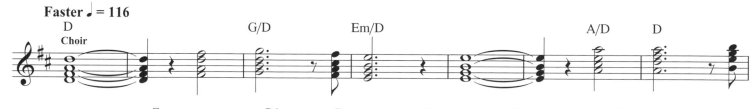

Slower ♩ = 105

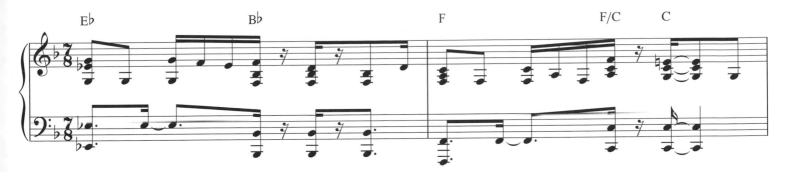

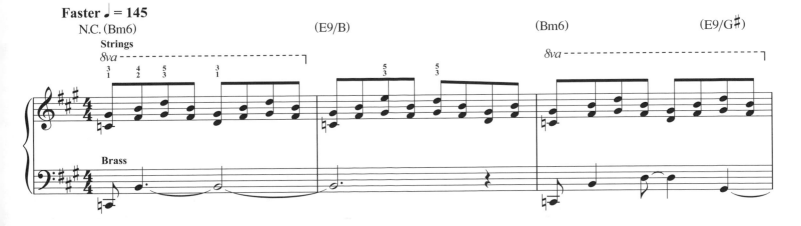

Slower ♩ = 112

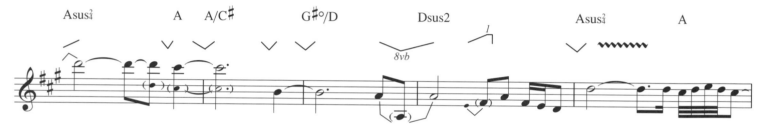

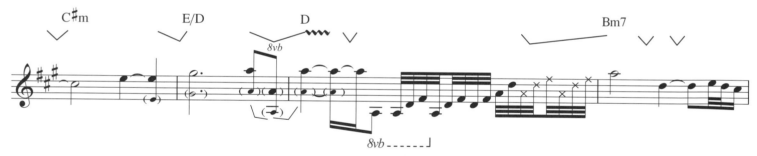

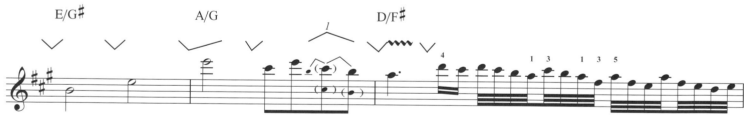

Free Time

Segue to "The Gift of Music"

The Gift of Music

Music by John Petrucci and Jordan Rudess
Lyrics by John Petrucci

Intro
Moderately Fast ♩ = 158

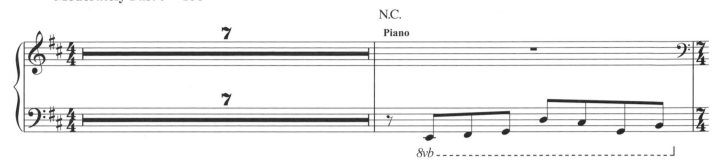

A

Em7add11

Verse
"Far in the distant future..."
A

Gsus2   Dadd9/G   A

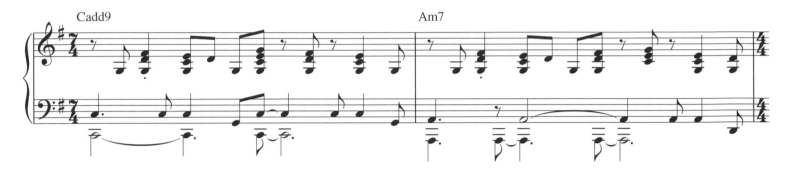

"Across the vast North Empire..."

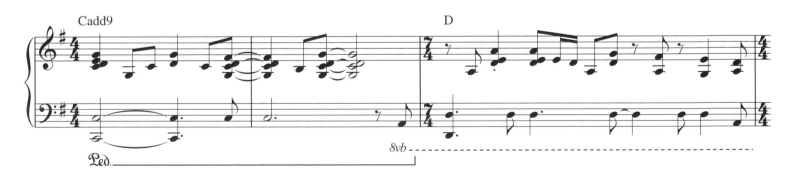

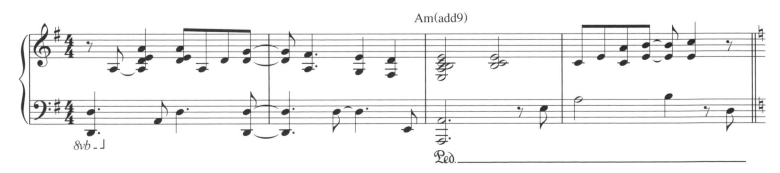

Bridge

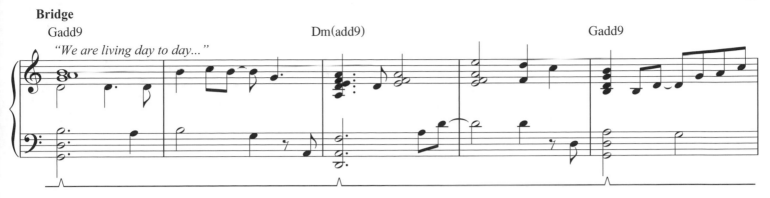

"We are living day to day..."

Verse

A

"There walks a God among us..."

Gsus2

D/G

Gadd9

A

Em7add11

D#°7

F#°7

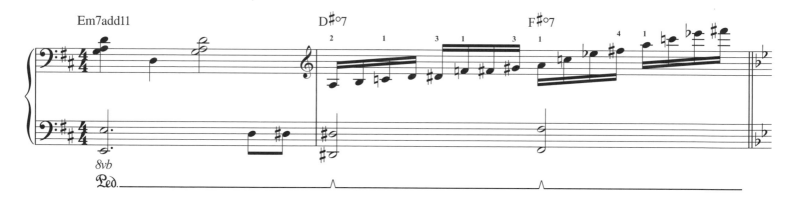

Chorus

Gm

Dm

Cadd9

F/A

"My brother Gabriel is all the hope we need..."

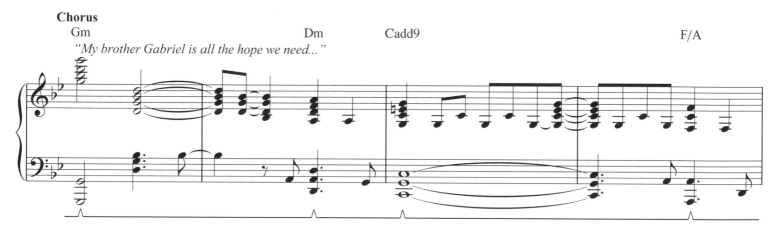

Gm

F/A

B♭6

Cadd9

Fmaj7/A

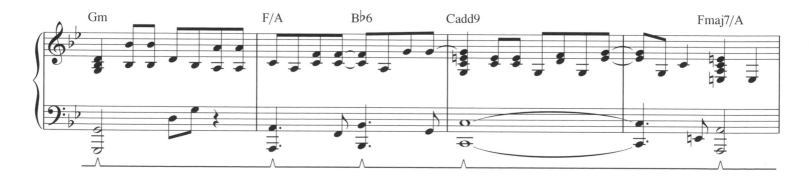

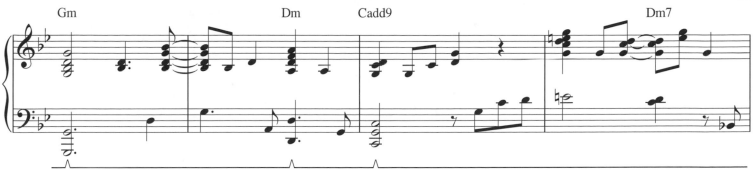

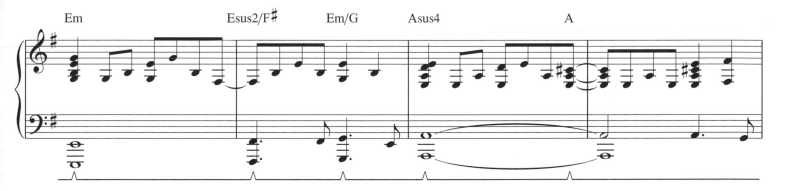

"*Music is the gift he brings...*"

Guitar Solo

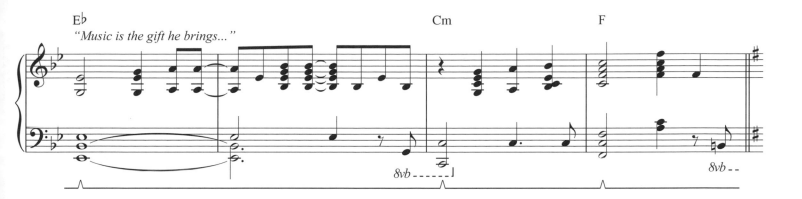

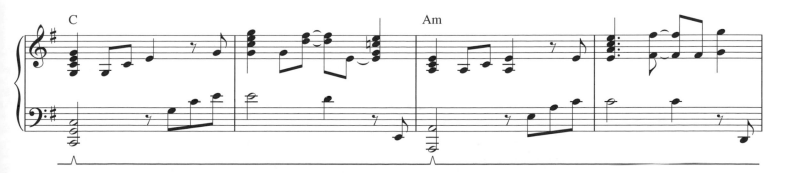

Interlude

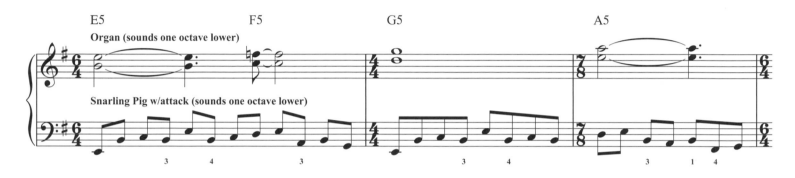

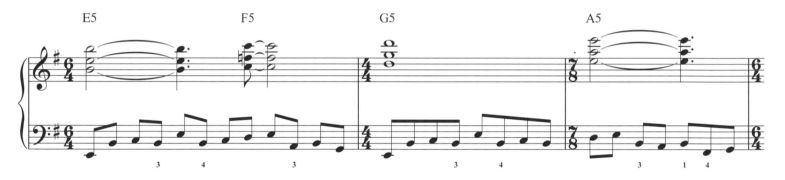

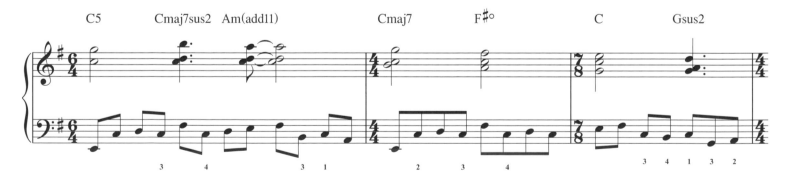

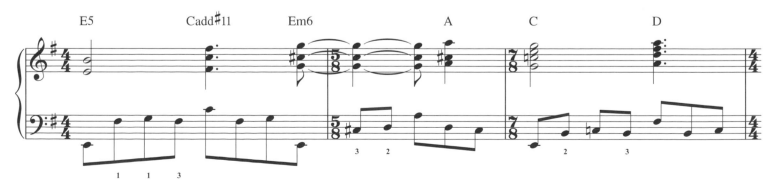

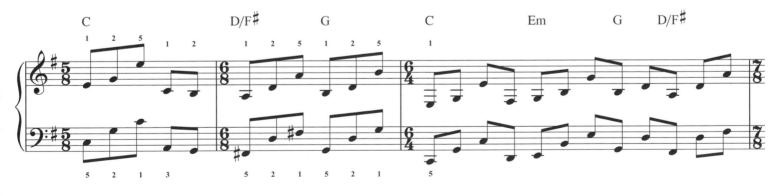

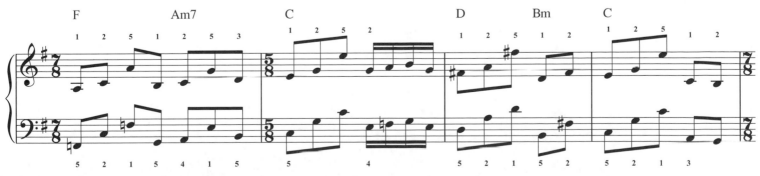

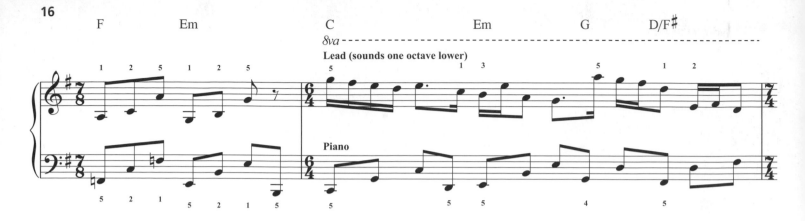

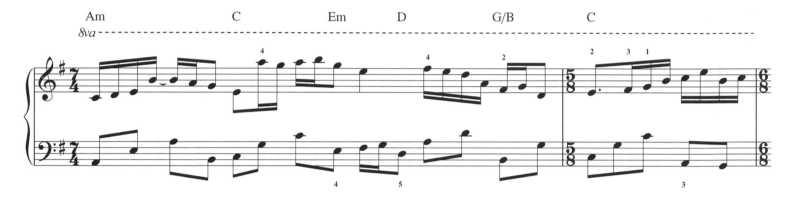

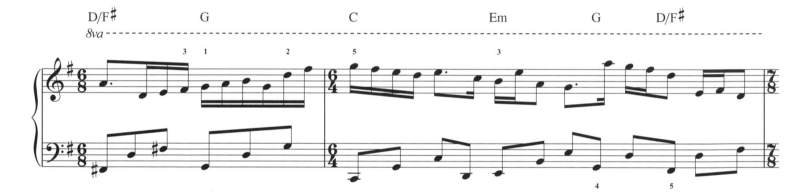

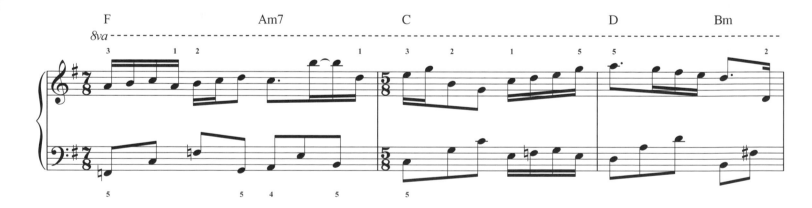

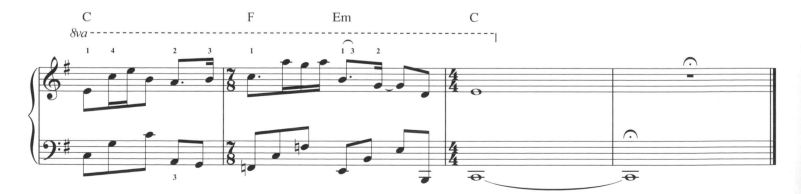

Lord Nafaryus

Music by John Petrucci and Jordan Rudess
Lyrics by John Petrucci

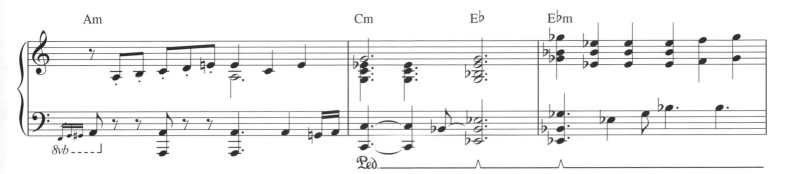

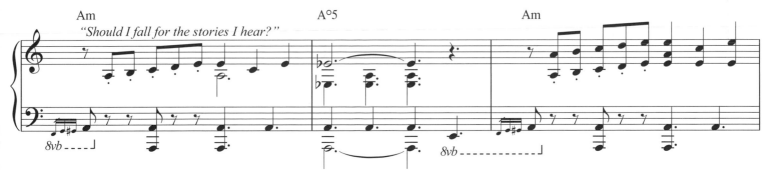

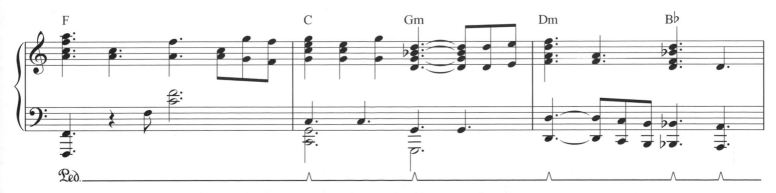

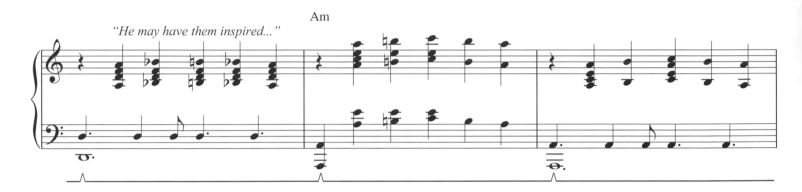

"He may have them inspired..."

"For myself I must see..."

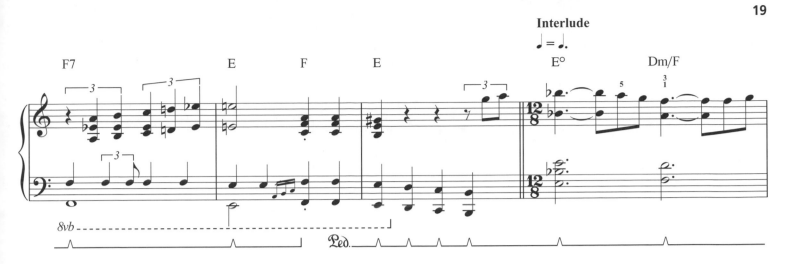

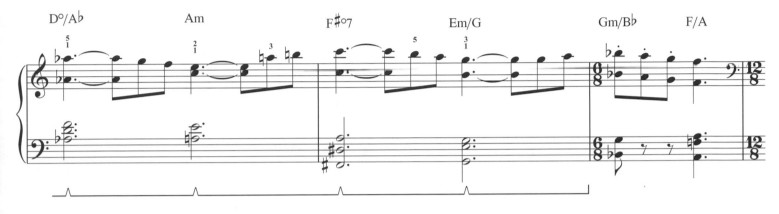

"I've heard the whispering..."

Bridge

A5   A

"His decision is made..."

Piano

Gm7   B♭

D°/A♭   A5   A

Dm   Gm   Dm/F   C/E

"In the coming days..."

F   C/E   B♭/D   E♭   Gm/D

Verse

"As a symbol of power and might..."

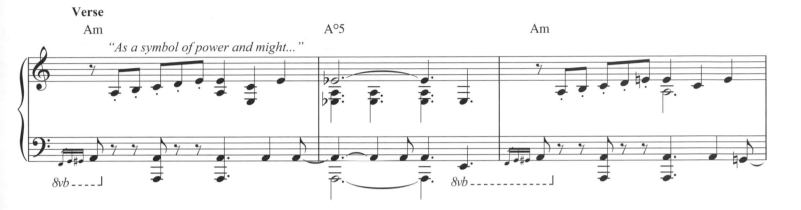

Chorus
Slower ♩ = 65

"Arabelle who means the
world to me..."

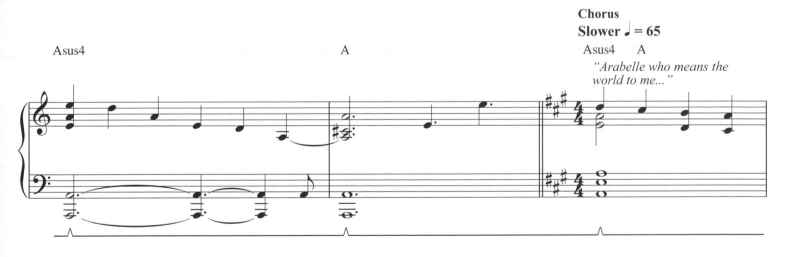

Outro

"Into the far off reaches of the land..."

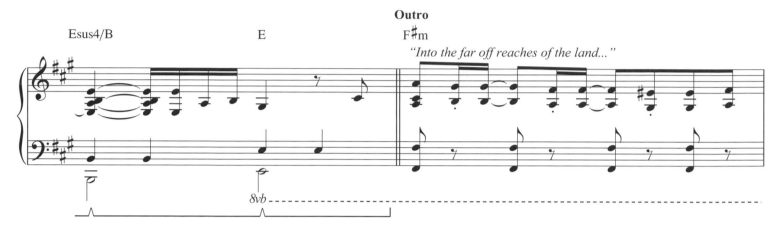

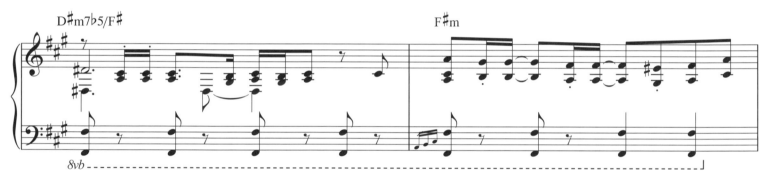

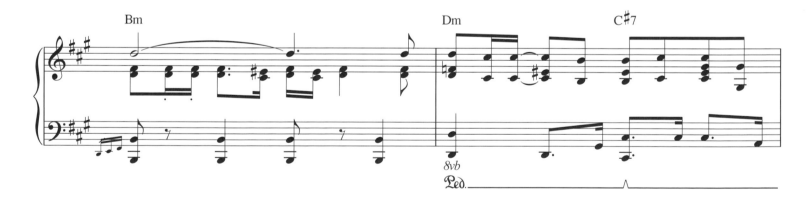

Freely (Slower)

"Yes we shall see."

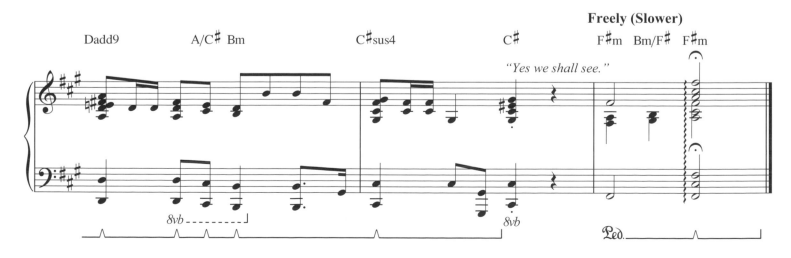

When Your Time Has Come

Music by John Petrucci and Jordan Rudess
Lyrics by John Petrucci

Bm7   Gsus2   Asus4

Verse

Dadd9   Aadd9   Gadd9

"When your time has come..."

Piano

Dadd9   G   Dadd9

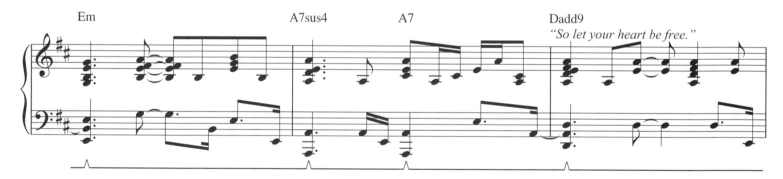

Em   A7sus4   A7   Dadd9

"So let your heart be free."

Aadd9   G   Dadd9

Gadd9   Em   Dadd9/A

Chorus

"When you're facing the path that divides..."

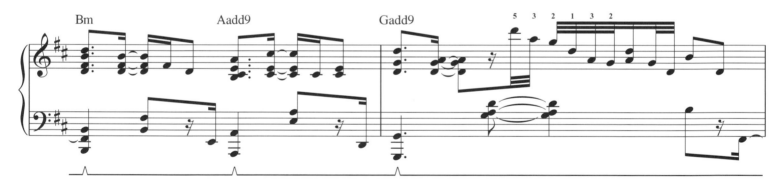

Guitar Solo

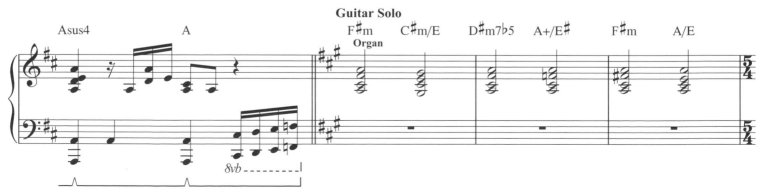

Three Days

Music by John Petrucci and Jordan Rudess
Lyrics by John Petrucci

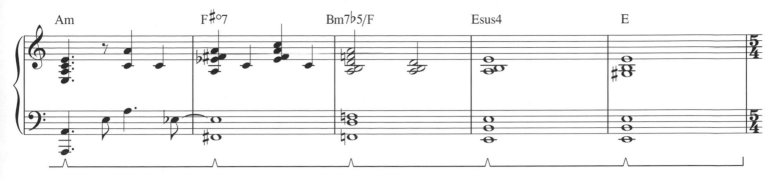

Moderately Fast ♩ = 160

Verse

"Need I remind you? I am the ruler here."

Pre-Chorus

"Hide and protect him, send him away..."

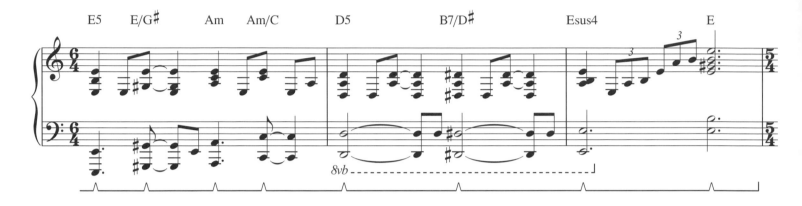

Chorus

"*Brace yourself. Bow down to Nafaryus.*"

Organ w/distortion

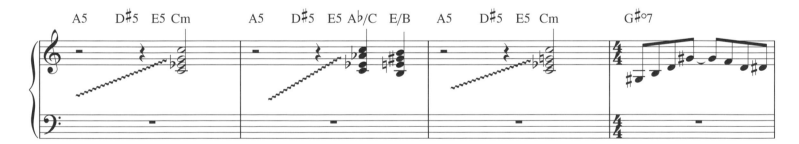

Verse

Half-time feel

"*He'll surrender on his own. If not, there'll be hell to pay.*"

Honky-tonk Piano

End half-time feel

Interlude

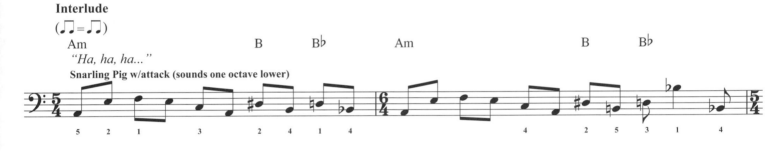

Pre-Chorus

"Send home the rebels, call off the fight..."

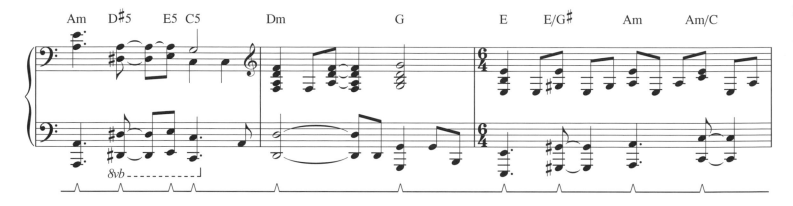

"Brace yourself. Bow down to Nafaryus."

Chorus

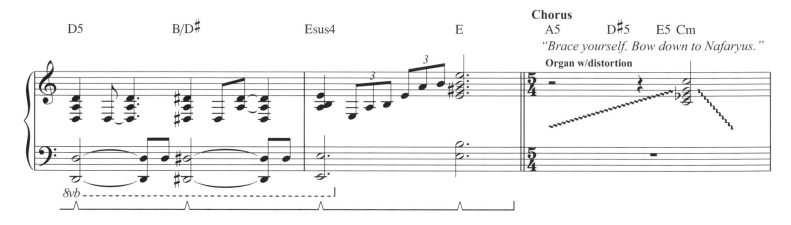

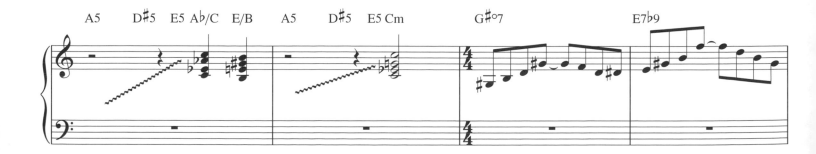

Outro
Slower ♩ = 118
Half-time feel

"With this frightening decree, Nafaryus departs."

Brass

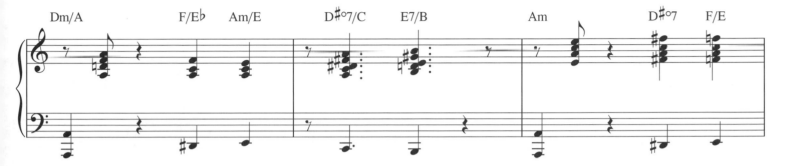

"Judgement Day will soon arrive in only three days' time."

Piano

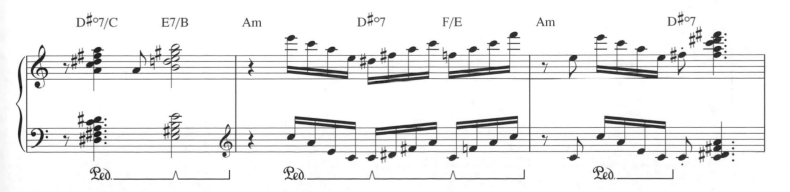

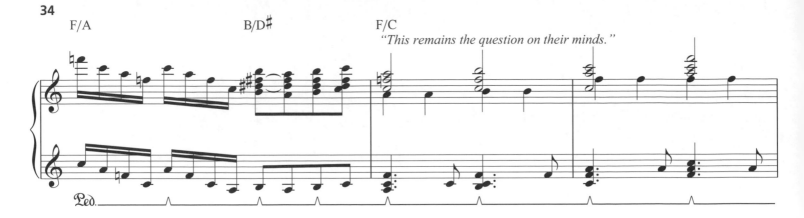

"This remains the question on their minds."

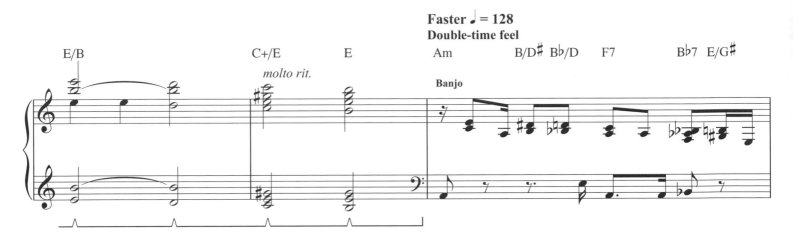

Faster ♩ = 128
Double-time feel

molto rit.

Banjo

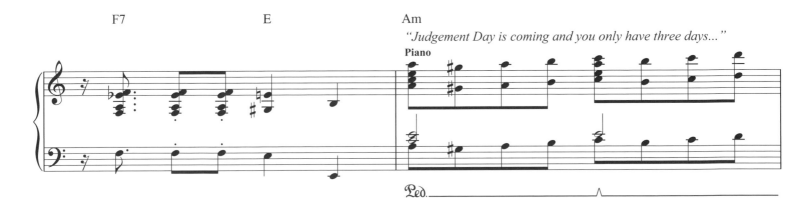

"Judgement Day is coming and you only have three days..."

Piano

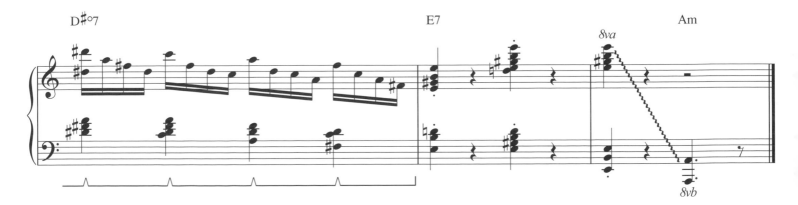

A Life Left Behind

Music by John Petrucci and Jordan Rudess
Lyrics by John Petrucci

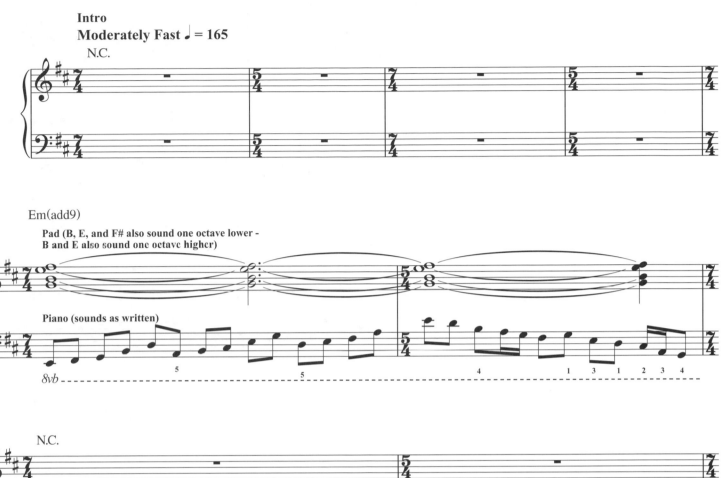

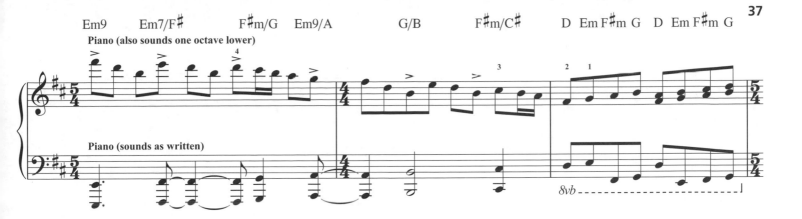

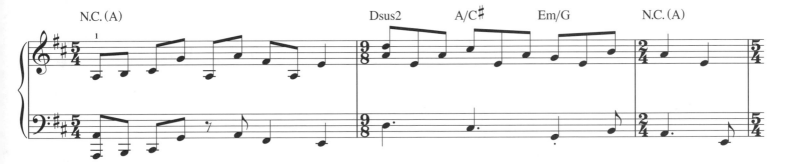

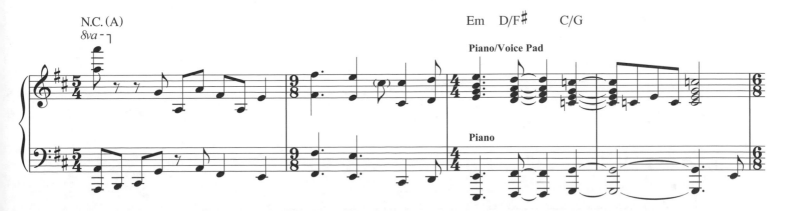

Verse

"I never knew someone was out there..."

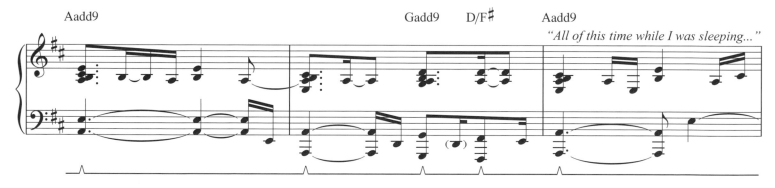

"All of this time while I was sleeping..."

Chorus

"I'm waking up from a life left behind..."

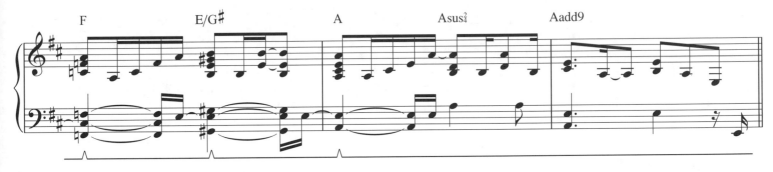

Verse

"Fate found a way to bring them together..."

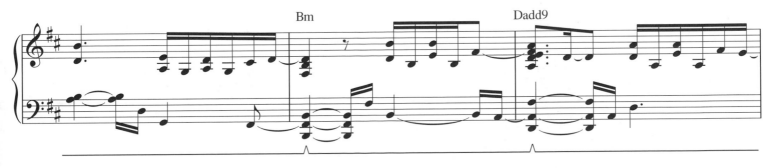

"Nothing I say can keep her from leaving..."

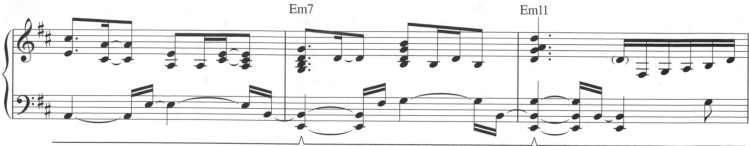

Em7　　　Em11

F　　　Em7　　　Aadd9

Chorus

"I'm waking up from a life left behind..."　　　Asus$^2_4$　　　A　　　Asus$^2_4$　　A

Em7　　　D/E　　　Em9　　　Dadd9

F　　　E7/G♯　　　Asus2　　　Asus$^2_4$　　　Aadd9

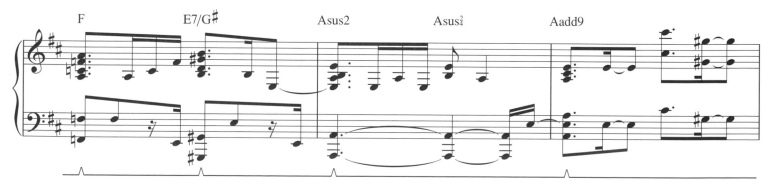

A　　　Asus$^2_4$　　　A　　　Asus$^2_4$　　A　　Em7　　　D/E

"I'm waking up now that yesterday's gone..."

Bridge

"I'll plan to return well disguised..."

Chorus

"I'm waking up from a life left behind..."

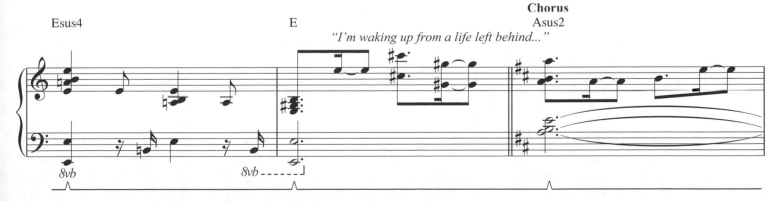

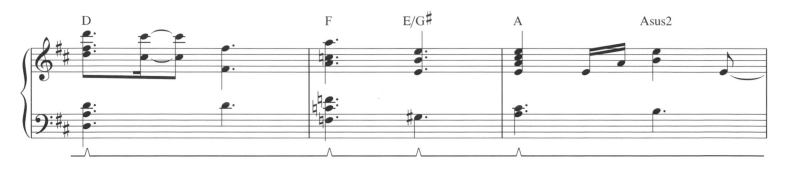

A

Asus2

A

"I'm waking up now that yesterday's gone..."

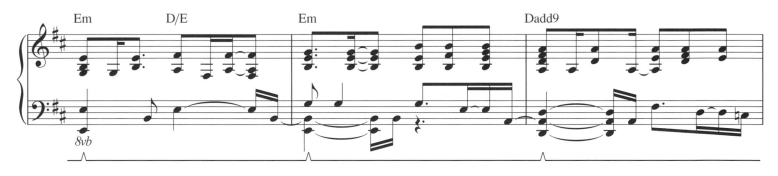

Outro

Em

Bm

Em

"You'll be her shadow as she moves, my son..."

"I'll keep her safe from all danger..."

Free Time

Ravenskill

Music by John Petrucci and Jordan Rudess
Lyrics by John Petrucci

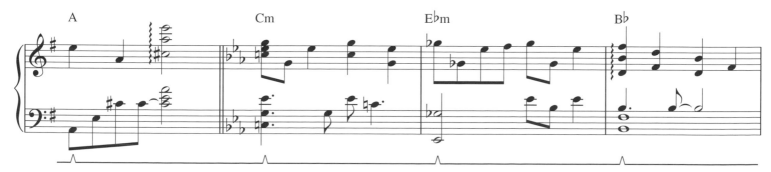

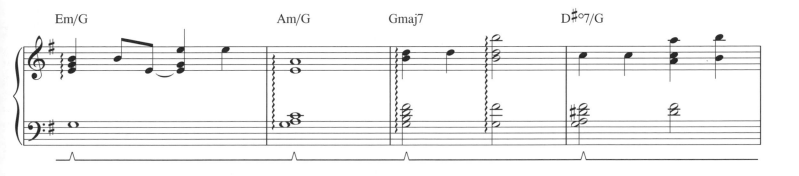

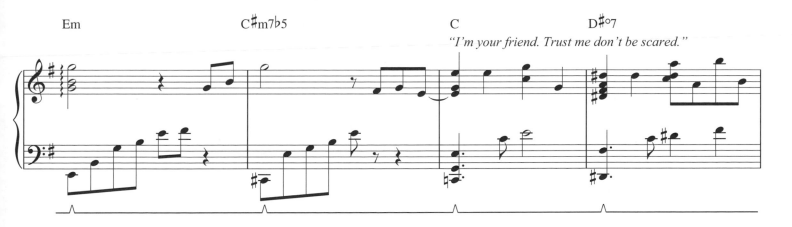

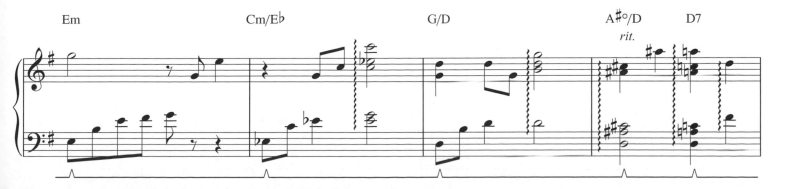

Slightly Faster ♩ = 84

Verse

"Hopeful and innocent, sensing no danger..."

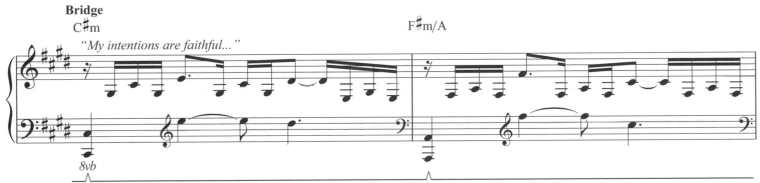

Bridge

"My intentions are faithful..."

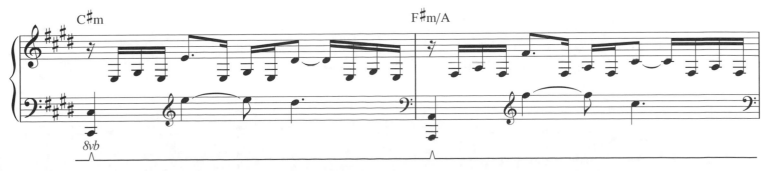

Bsus4   B

8vb

Chorus
Em

"You dare to stand before my eyes..."

A   D   G5   Em

         Am   Bsus4   B   C#m

D5add9   Bm   E/G#   E   **Interlude**
                                                  D

"Lost in this moment..."

Bm   C#m   E

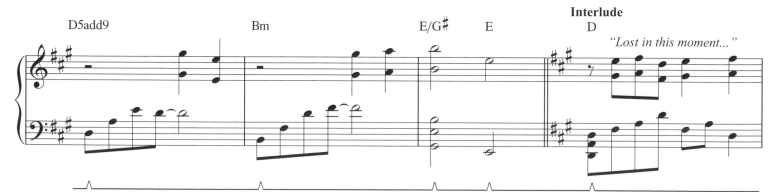

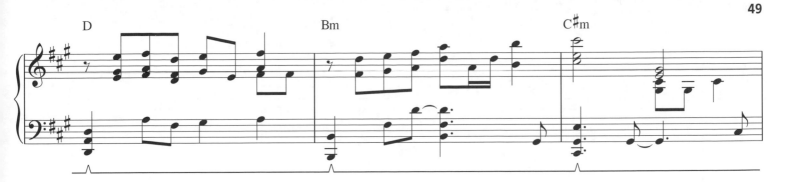

"I would wait a lifetime just to see your face..."

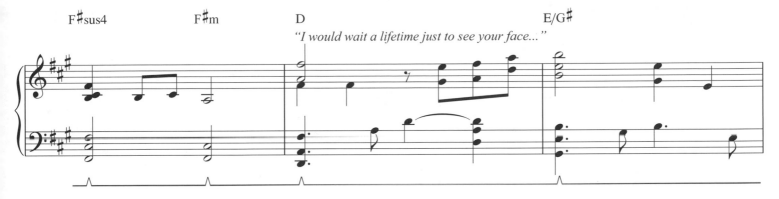

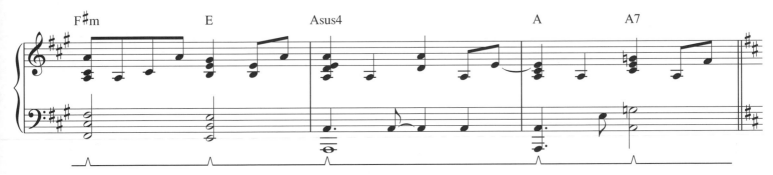

Outro

"I remember your father was moved by my song..."

"We will walk this road together..."

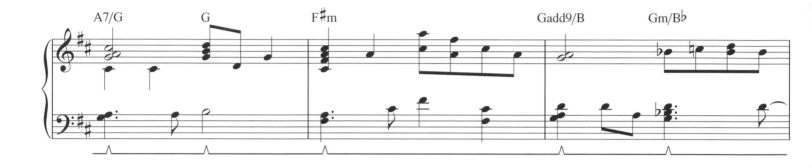

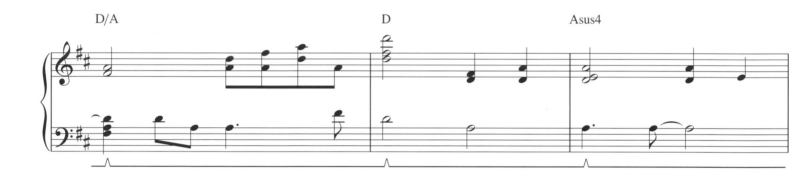

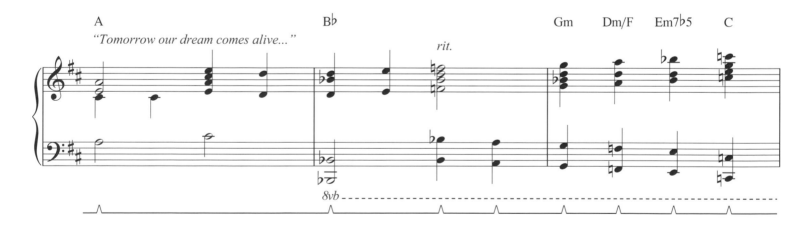

"Tomorrow our dream comes alive..."

Free Time

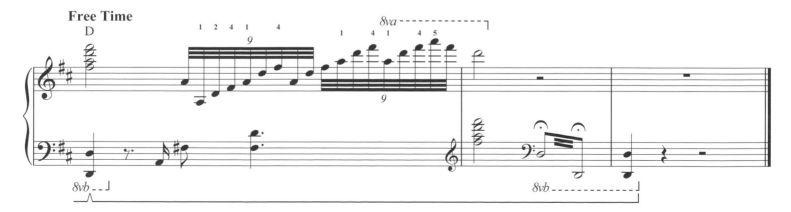

A Tempting Offer

Music by John Petrucci and Jordan Rudess
Lyrics by John Petrucci

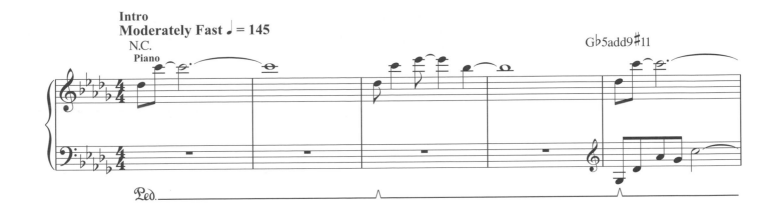

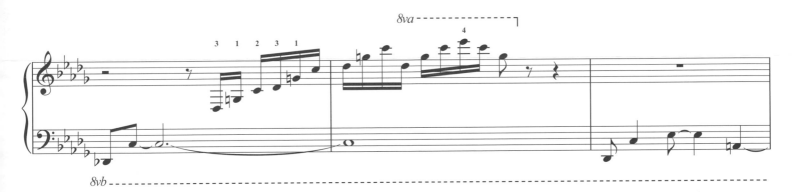

Chorus

"How dare you step inside my home!"

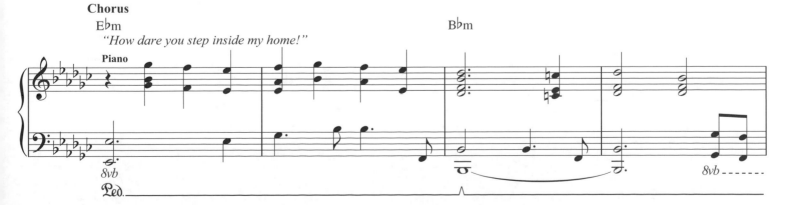

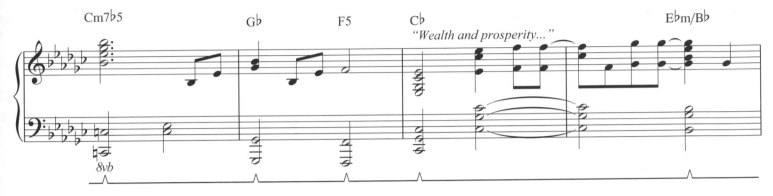

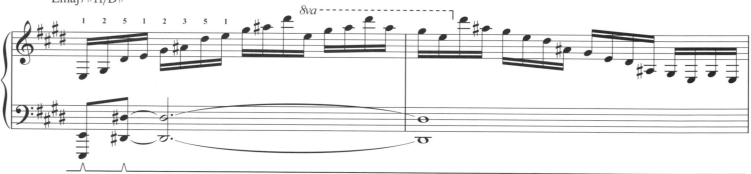

Bridge
Slower ♩ = 136

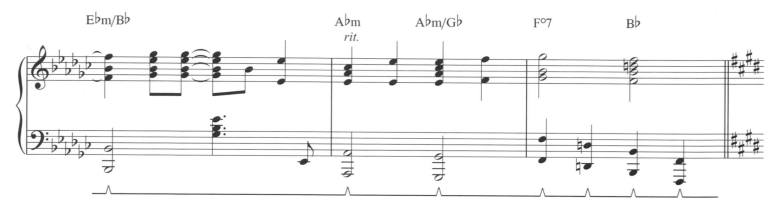

"I am through with being pushed aside..."

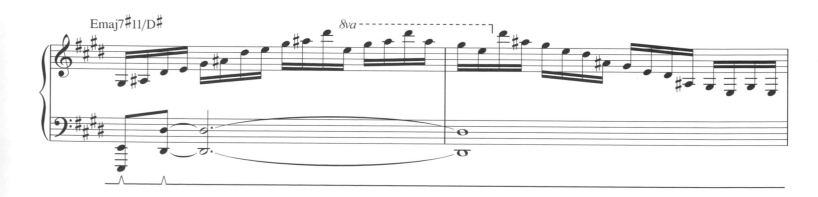

C7♭9♭13

N.C.

"Take the evening to decide."
molto rit.

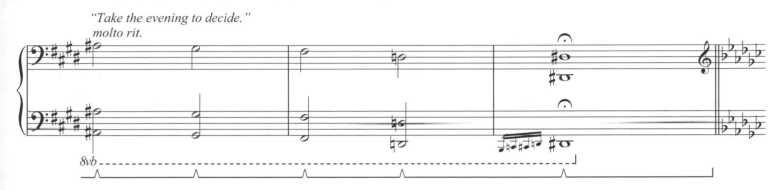

Outro
Rubato ♩ = 140

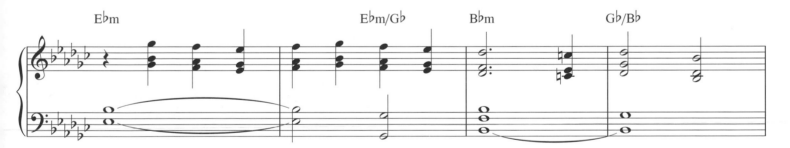

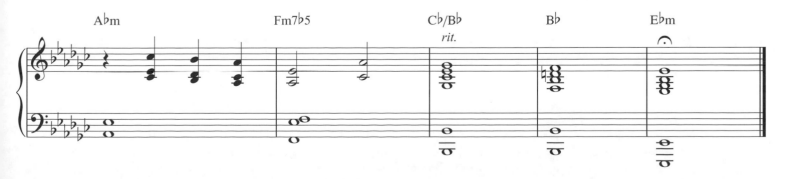

A New Beginning

Music by John Petrucci and Jordan Rudess
Lyrics by John Petrucci

Intro
Moderately ♩ = 110
N.C. (G5)

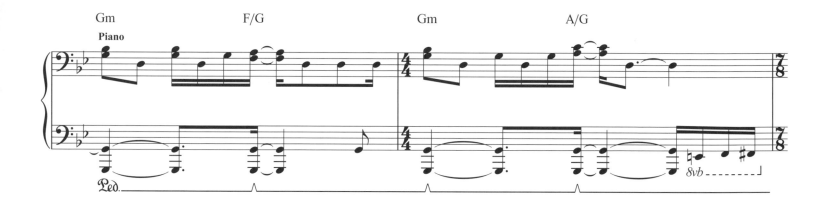

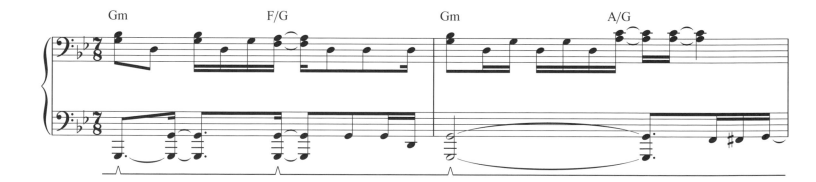

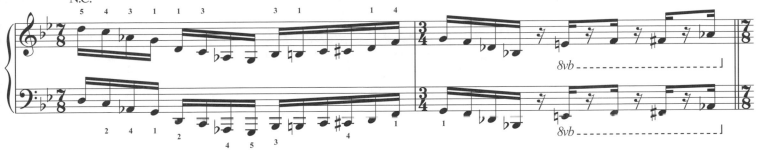

Verse

"Father, I implore you, don't believe a word..."

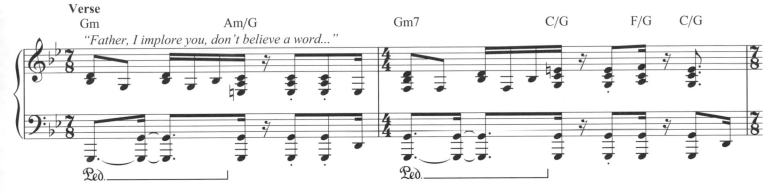

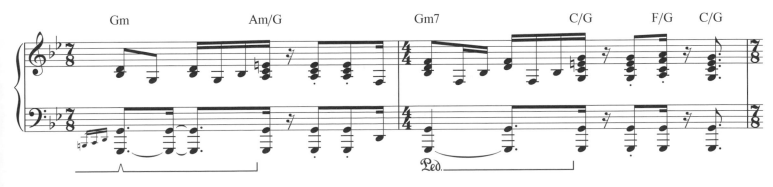

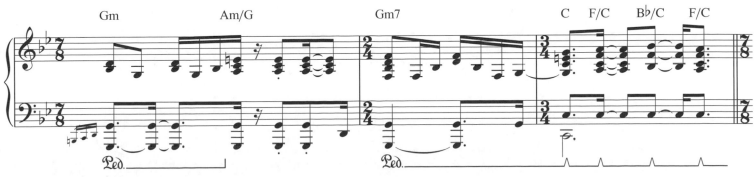

Chorus

"Give us both a chance for a new beginning..."

Bridge

"This man's a fraud and a hoax..."

Verse

"Ignorant and stubborn, you have no respect..."

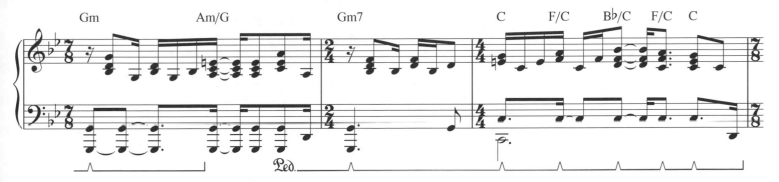

Chorus

"We don't stand a chance. That is his opinion..."

62

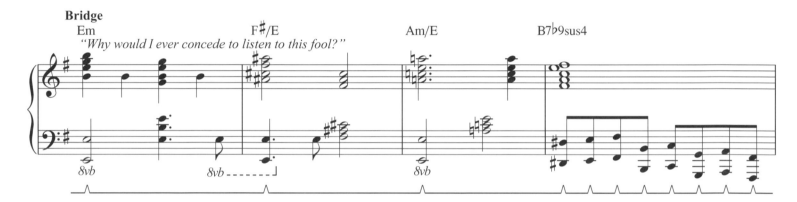

Bridge

Interlude

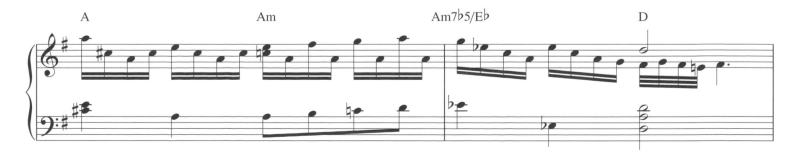

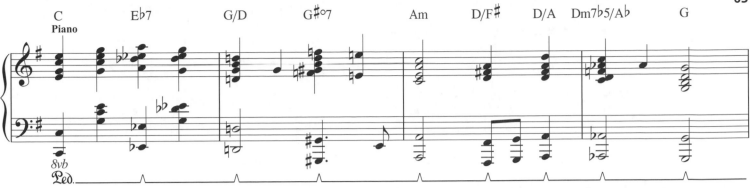

Verse

"Not long ago, there was a time and place..."

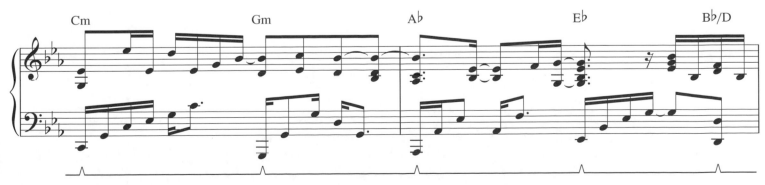

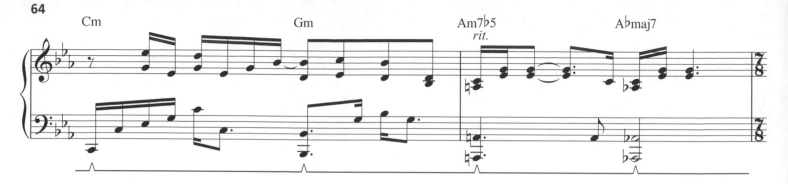

Faster ♩ = 110

"Father, is it true..."

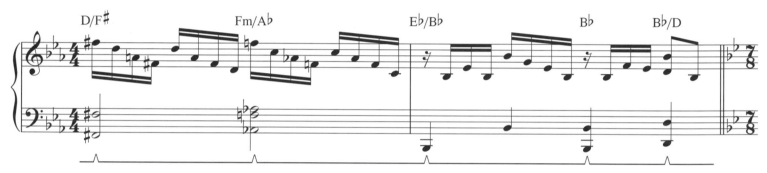

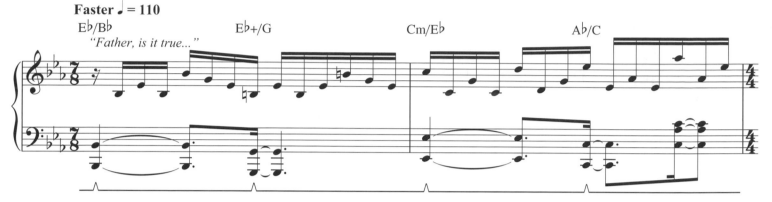

Chorus

"Now you understand why I was hiding..."

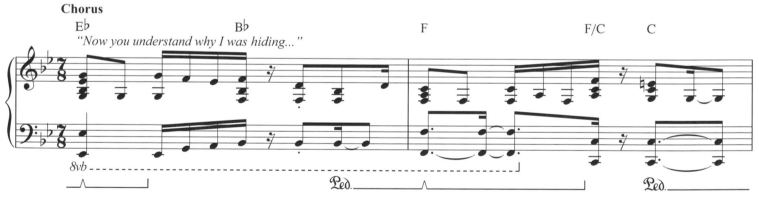

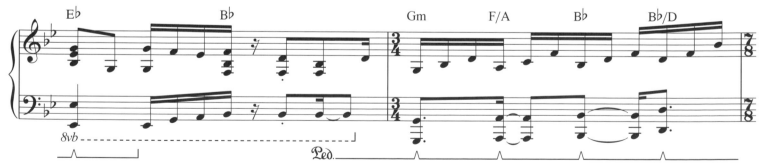

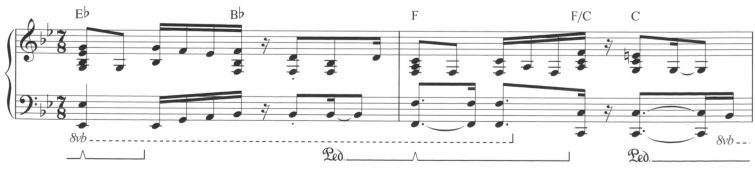

Synth Solo

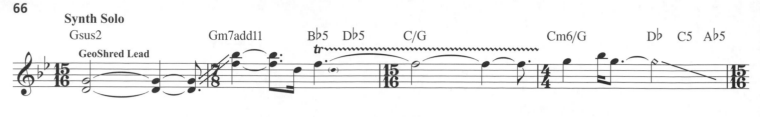

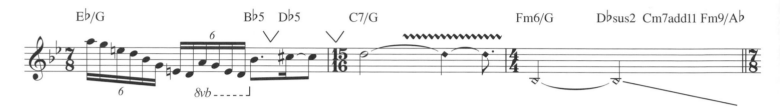

Interlude

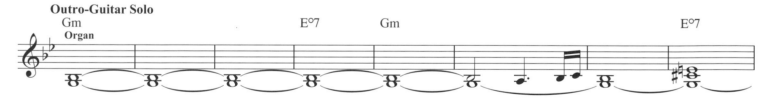

Outro-Guitar Solo

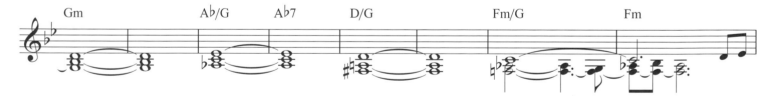

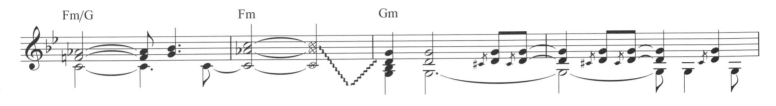

Begin fade

Fade out

Moment of Betrayal

Music by John Petrucci and Jordan Rudess
Lyrics by John Petrucci

Intro
Moderately Fast ♩ = 163

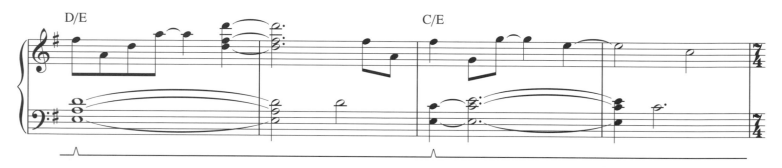

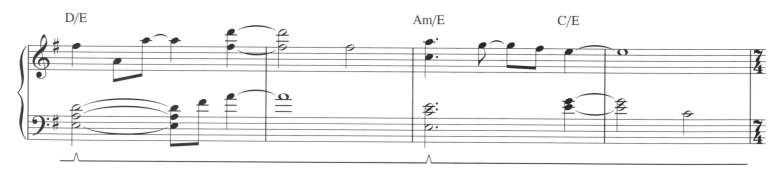

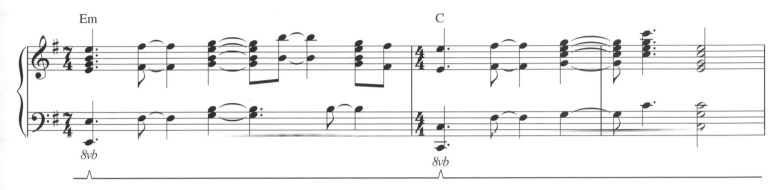

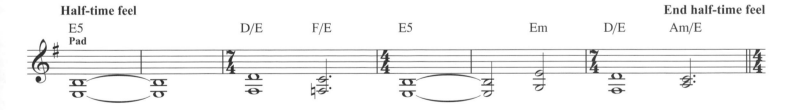

Pre-Chorus

Chorus

Verse

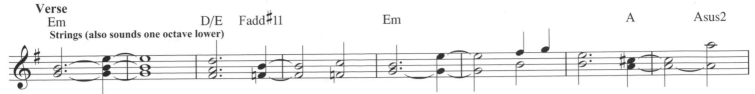

Pre-Chorus

Chorus

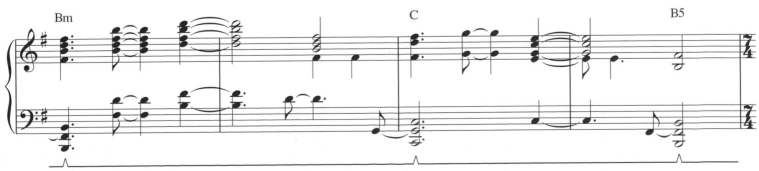

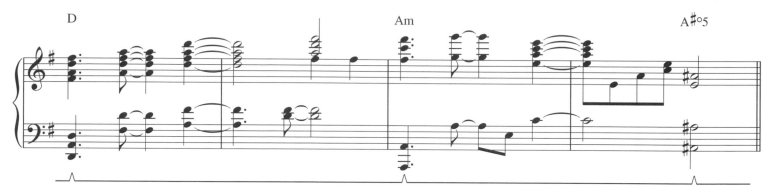

Bridge

Interlude

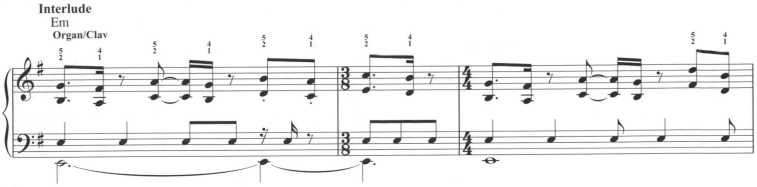

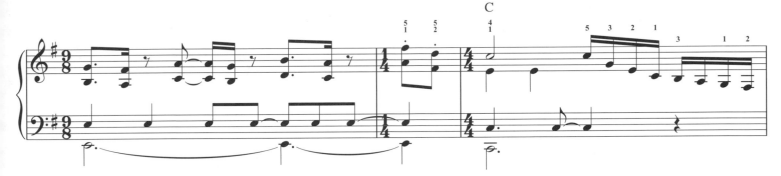

(B)

Guitar Solo
Half-time feel

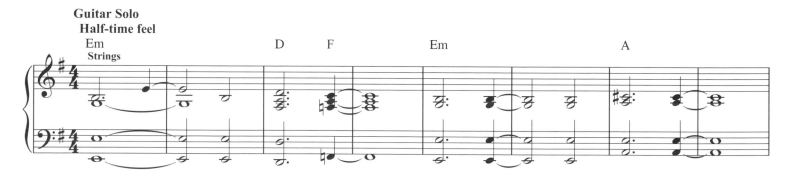

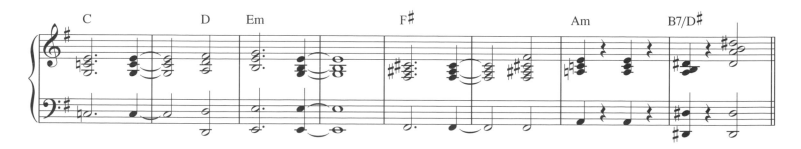

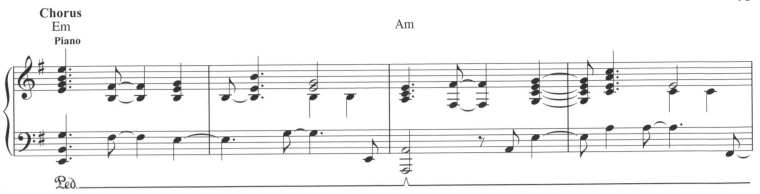

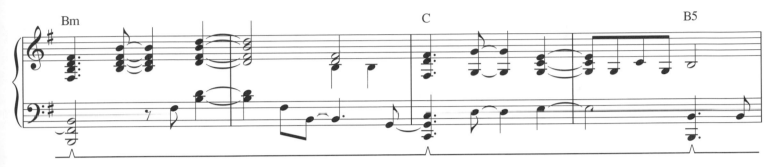

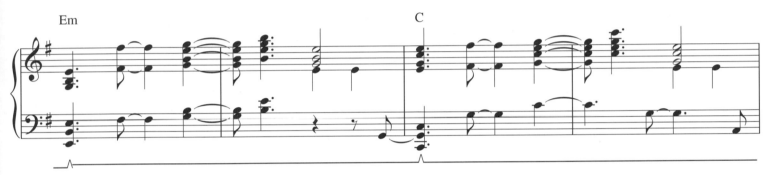

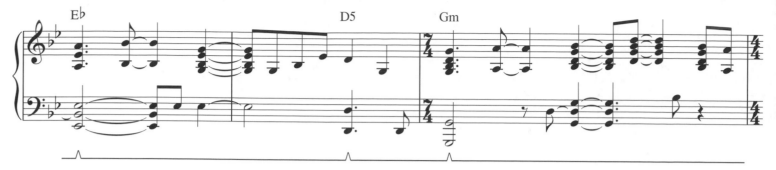

Outro
Half-time feel

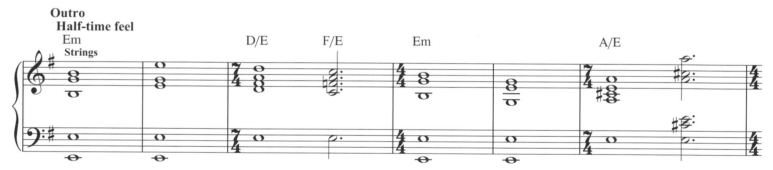

Heaven's Cove

Music by John Petrucci and Jordan Rudess
Lyrics by John Petrucci

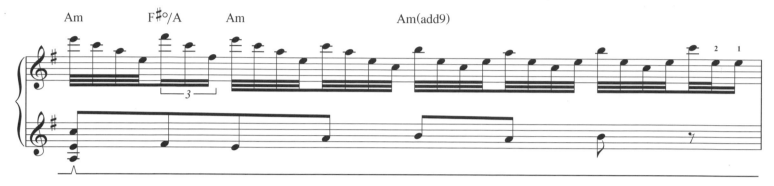

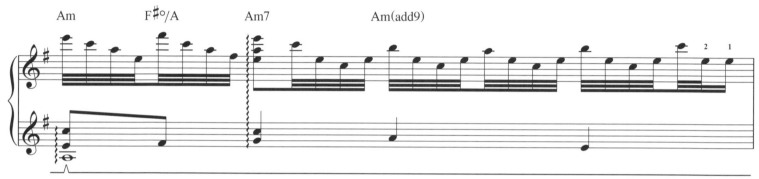

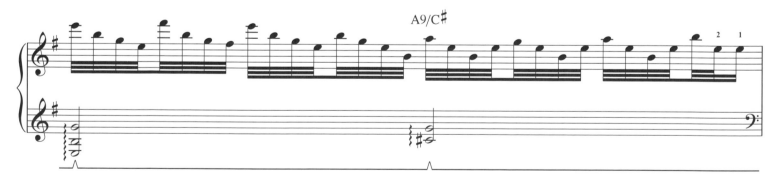

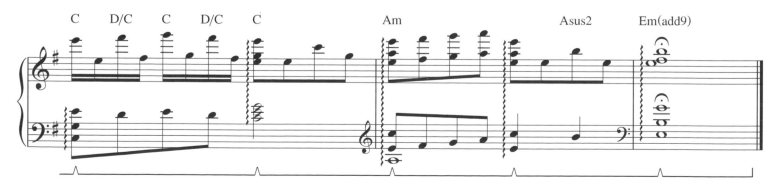

The Path That Divides

Music by John Petrucci and Jordan Rudess
Lyrics by John Petrucci

Bridge

F#m

"Ahrys was never aware his son had followed him there..."

Bm/D

F#m/E

Bm

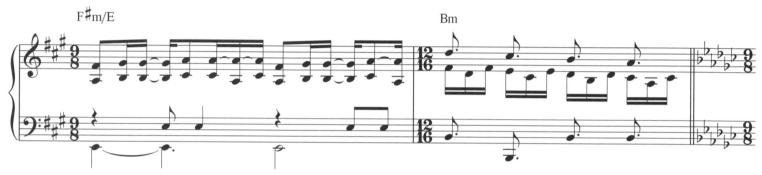

Ebm

Abm/Cb

Ebm/Db

Cb   Ebm/Bb   Gb   Ebm

Chorus

E   G#m   B   D#m   E

"On the path that divides, you are there by my side..."

Strings

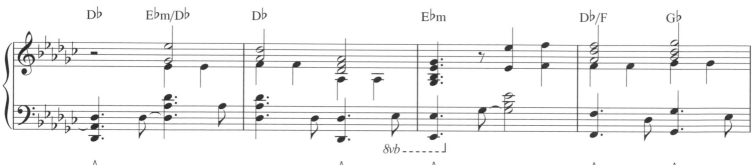

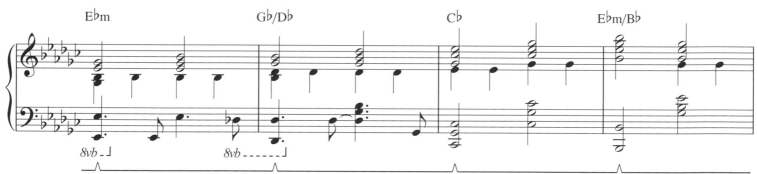

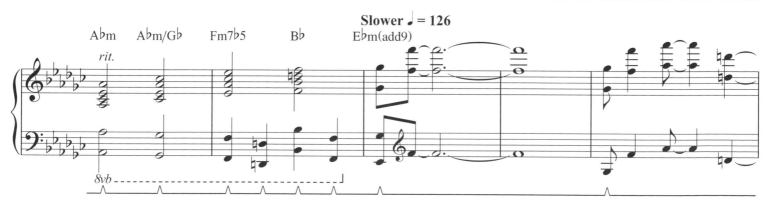

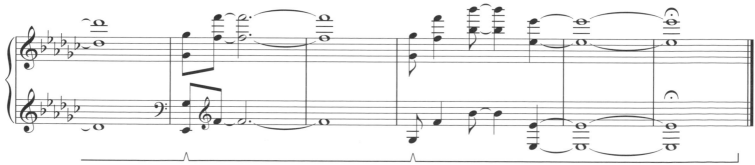

The Walking Shadow

Music by John Petrucci and Jordan Rudess
Lyrics by John Petrucci

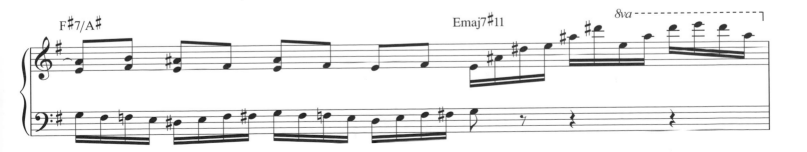

Interlude

Verse
Half-time feel

"Don't hold your breath. The night's still young."

End half-time feel

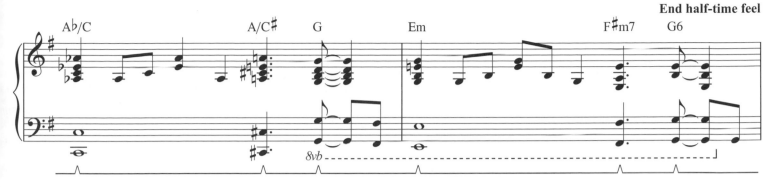

Interlude
Half-time feel

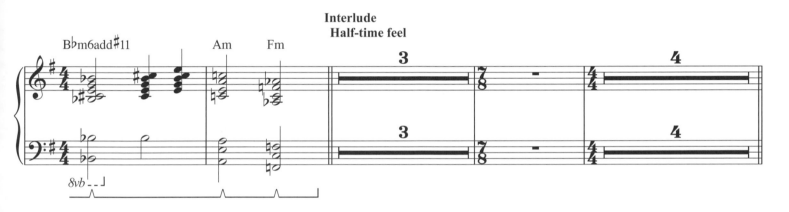

Chorus

"Drawing closer pace by pace..."

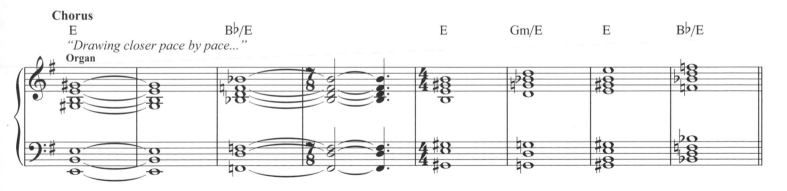

Interlude

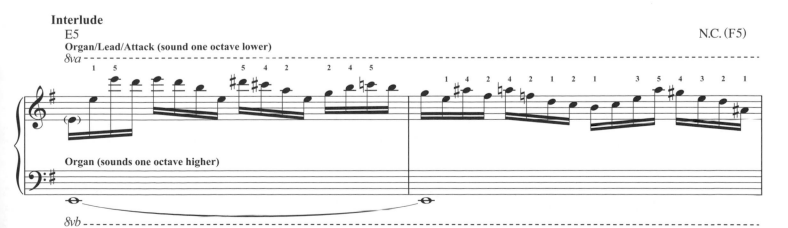

My Last Farewell

Music by John Petrucci and Jordan Rudess
Lyrics by John Petrucci

Verse

"Have I wandered into someone's nightmare?"

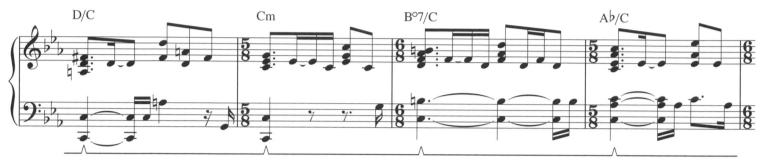

Keyboard Solo

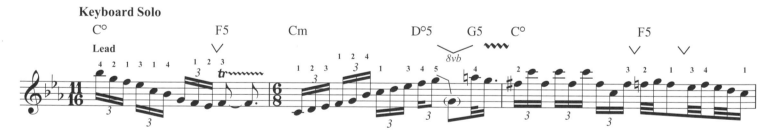

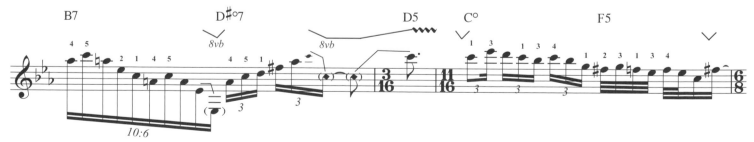

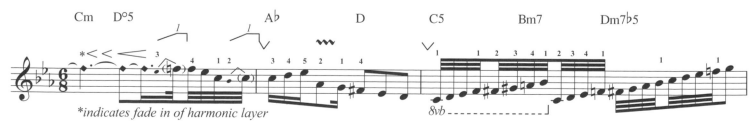

indicates fade in of harmonic layer

Chorus

"Don't leave me now."

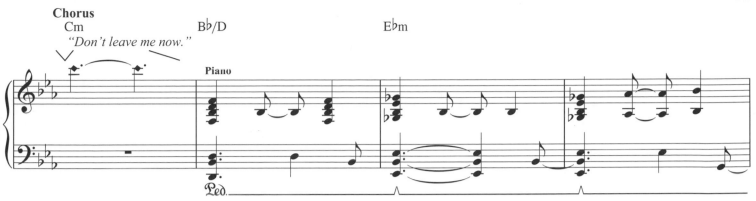

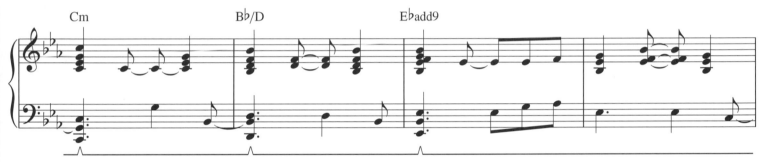

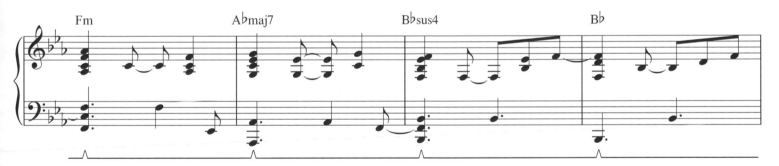

"All your life you have walked alone."

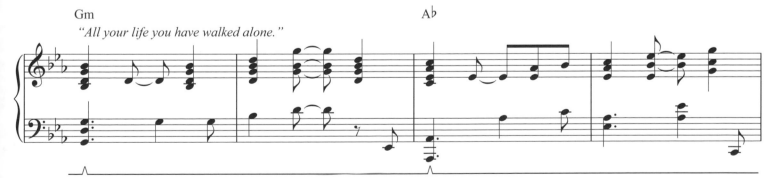

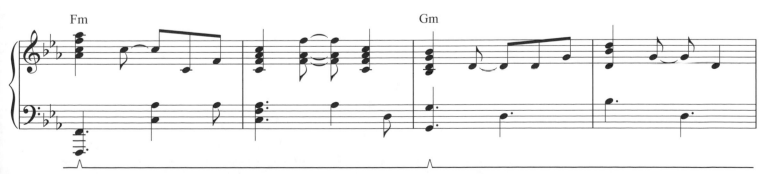

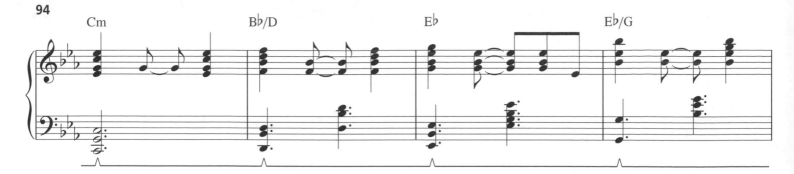

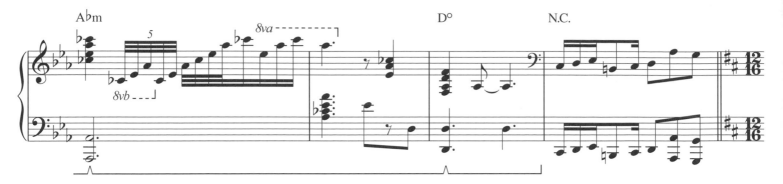

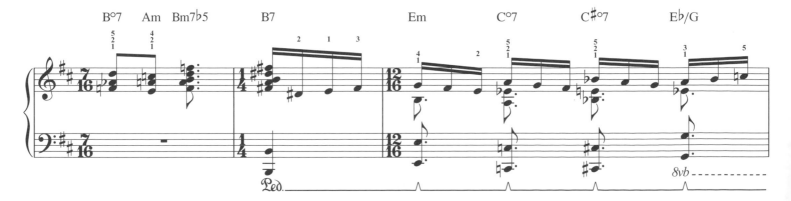

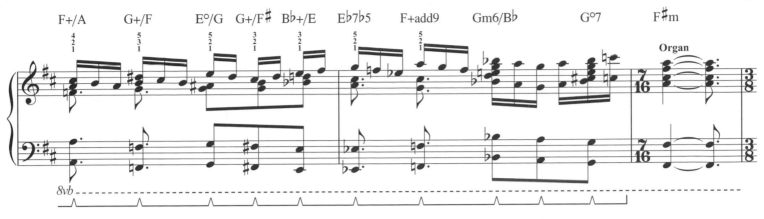

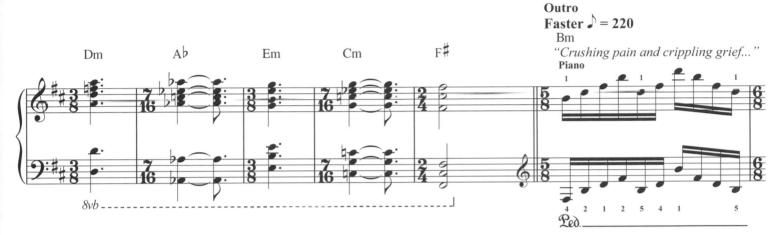

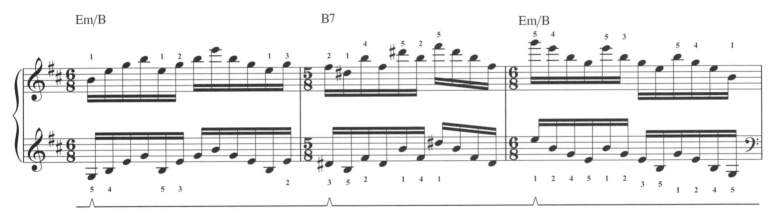

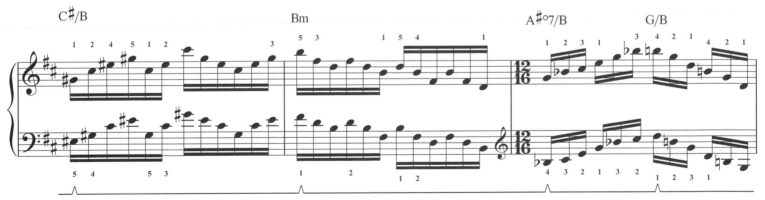

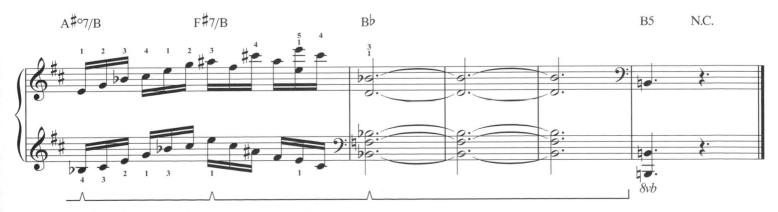